WALKING TOOTH & CLOUD

WALKING TOOTH & CLOUD

Albert Flynn DeSilver

French Connection Press • Paris • 2007

Published by FRENCH CONNECTION PRESS
12 rue Lamartine, 75009 Paris, France

FRENCH CONNECTION PRESS books are distributed in the
U.S. by Small Press Distribution (www.spdbooks.org)
and Baker & Taylor.

www.frenchcx.com

Walking Tooth & Cloud

ISBN: 978-2-914853-08-8

Infinite thanks to Eric Ellena and Ian Ayers, editors and publishers of
FRENCH CONNECTION PRESS books and *Van Gogh's Ear* magazine.
All photos, cover, layout and design by AFD
The author wishes to thank the editors and publishers of the following
magazines in which these poems first appeared:

*Luna, Fishdrum, Columbia Poetry Review, Combo, Conduit, Realpoetik, Van
Gogh's Ear, Puppy Flowers, Zyzzyva, Exquisite Corpse, Untitled, Web del Sol,
Prosodia, Lungfull!,* and *can we have our ball back.*

Some of these poems also appeared in a chapbook titled *Ageless in Sleep*
with drawings by Neil Osborn, published in Colorado Springs by Angry
Dog Midget Editions (# 11), 2002. Thanks to Noel Black. Thanks also to
Fulcrum Media. Eternal love and thanks to Marian.

Printed in the U.S.A.

Contents

for Magpie & Serena

WALKING TOOTH & CLOUD

THE PODIUM

The poet approaches the podium. Once there, he bows and grabs firmly each wooden edge like a bull by the horns—so much so that it becomes a bull's head and horns, no longer a mere simile but the real thing. He is in Pamplona, the crowd shouts "Trompa de lirio por las verdes ingles!" (Horn of the lily through green groins!) In the ring he stumbles among crushed wax cups, hot dogs, and roses, addressing the frenzied crowd with his terror, his poems now woven into a single red cloth. He is chased viciously around the ring, tormented with imminent mockery or even worse the idea of his death. He is soon pinned against the far wall, face to face with the bull's nostrils, which are spewing forth ash from the incinerated bodies of small children. In an instant of blind fright the man lunges and grabs the bull by the horns, like the square, ferocious edges of a podium—where he greets the audience with his first poem, called "The Podium."

THE SCULPTRESS IN THE FIRST PLACE

She kept George's ashes in the Curious George shopping bag on the particle board bookshelf, in between the children's books. Whenever she missed him terribly, she would lean over the bag and weep into it as if to try and water him back to life.

One time, overcome with the depths of her grief while standing over the bag, tears streaming—she reached in and scooped up a handful of ash, its granular weight a palm full of wet cement. She began shaping and sculpting him back into a man, a small clay replica of the George she once knew. She molded his head with the inside of her fist. With long magenta fingernails she carved his nervous eyes, spiral ears, hooked nose, and thin mouth, that favorite raised scar across his chin. She rolled his legs between her fingers, shaped his torso between sad palms—adhering all limbs with her weak saliva. Soon he was ready to be set in the oven (yet again), as she would a delicate pie. At this point he spoke up through the tiny slit she had inlaid for a mouth, his voice whistling through the tiny bone crumbs of his teeth.

"I am no longer one of your fucking baked goods!" he shouted. "I have already been clothed in the sun, this is redundant—its overrated & overheated, and besides I'm due to re-nourish the soil, pay back the plants that have so furthered my growing. Shaping me into a more permanent form robs me of my curiosity—why not just seed me into the passing cloud that I am?"

"But my grief permits me only sculpture, and curiosity is what killed the cat, the monkey, the man in the first place," she cried, cranking the oven to 550.

NINE WINDOWS

A man walks out of a cumulus-flooded apple with a nine-pane window painted on his impossible sternum, his torso steaming at the woody core. You can see the nine scars of light through his bone. He counts off the scars on each finger. Not knowing what to do with the one finger extra, he hacks it off against the moon's crescent blade. The single finger is left to worm its way home through the turreted orchard, where it sits in the shade drawing clouds and apples in the grass.

CIRCLES

The dead ride our fingerprints in everything we touch, transient mazes never truly washing off. Each object spirit knots, and then there's air. Add waters, which take mazes to task in meandering, fluid tooth, the rivers chew. Each unstrung print is a musical score, an empty-tennis-racket snowshoe ancestral walkthrough. Try and unstring it by understanding and you'll get barked at by ancient maze-goers going haywire in your hands. Some are perched in a handkerchief, on the light switch, the refrigerated handle, and of course at the tip of the tap, where the waters curl. The doorknob is your steering wheel, where a clusterfuck of ancestry circles.

THE CANDLE

On a lank and crispy winter night, in a mountain town called Waxen Springs, a man settles down to a hearty bowl of steaming yellow soup. It is thickening as he drinks, as his thoughts and the mountains around him thicken. He soon realizes that it is not soup he spoons within him but rather a mirror of wax rapidly solidifying. Soon he is asleep. His mouth now propped open and tilted toward heaven, a small wick sprouts up between his teeth. After dinner his wife comes in to kiss him good night, but instead lights the wick and kisses the flame.

DEER LAWN CHAIR

Off I am to stroll in the woods as often I am found to do. Today it's quite wet, February storm just clearing, mist steaming gently off the dense pines. Along the muddy trail I slog, gun in hand, soon spotting a deer in the distance. I approach cautiously, gun braced against my shoulder. The deer stays put. I get even closer, within arms length in fact, and the deer, frightened beyond capacity, instead of sprinting off, folds in half like a lawn chair. I put the gun aside and take a seat, resting my arms on her thinly furred and stiffened legs. I lean back against her warm white belly and relax into watching the mist watching me, and after a good rest rise with it, folding up the lawn chair, prancing home.

CYPRESSES

A woman is hanging from a blind woman's clothesline. Sleeves emptying their raised shirts. The edge of the road is a raised shirt lining the sky. Other women are preening crows along the roadway, the way the sky is preening the road now folded in the clouds.

Cypresses had stolen an old man's hat when he came upon the line. The women were originally young of hand, had clasped books in their linens. Quiet were the nightbirds in their dresses, aroused was the old man in the cypress. All were afraid of each other, the slightly nudging wind. To navigate toward attempts would be fruitless—unless the cypress tops could be seen as fruit, and they could, being all clustered with the foliage of men and women and their linens.

"The evening is the master of levitation, is threadbare fruit," says the old man to the horizon line, watching it squirm.

THE BLIND MAN'S WIFE

After R.E.

The eternal clouds are the wife of looking, said the seer. The world is the husband of the air, said the blind man. The wife said, I am a statuesque roof beam in an archeologist's temple of dreams. I will kiss you then, swiftly, via roof-bound somersaults, and exit through the neck of your dress, crooned the archeologist. An overturned boat is the bottom of the sky, is the place from which I listen, said the wife. This central room is full of kissing, floating windows, and diving-backward husbands, said the seer. Form and reform the clouds into archeologist-looking wives, said the husband, facing a ridge of extremes from which the blind man fell through the eternal clouds. Ahhh, my wife, thought the blind man, looking his way forever inward.

THE FOGGY SCALP

Out to sea this evening I watch the horizon line buckle and snap under the weight of the setting sun. Two distinct green sticks collapse inward towards each other, pulling in the drowning sea. Only to be replaced by a single sky made of matted hair and skin cells in octagonal patches. This sure baffles the captain and his deck hands, who have run aground in the great scalp with the wrong tool for the job. Now during those long crossings they just sit around scratching themselves, staring into the foggy scalp.

CANOEING UP STAIRS

Oaks of stillness under bedrooms—a family by day—glides and seems to darken the quiet, injuring care—gently with paddles—dip we the upstairs hall in waters—quieting the final meditation—less an end like earth—in the deep, dripping fedoras, umbrellas, caved-in galoshes and overcoats dark with the weight of feeling. Could the upstairs closet the downstairs? Overpassing we & then?

Movie in a backward playpen—stairs falling down someone—feet slippered like they were and someone's bedroom remembered—doubt finding no step—flipping us past salmon—several meetings of them in the banisters. In paddling my catchings I kept a canoe—for the going up of stairs.

THE SCENE IS THE END

The scene is topped with clouds and steam, blurring an archway where a pair of crossed hands emerge from a leaden egg. I find it to be my very own, the only lead egg I'll ever birth. The soft metallic shell peels away like damp pages, laid round upon some neatly patterned cobblestone. It is lit gently from within. The handy egg is rolled to the foot of a wrought iron gate and wrings darkness through its wrought iron fingers. The end.

KAFKA'S TWO-HANDED WAR

Approval is met by me nodding. Me nodding being a dishonest referee. I am watching my two hands at arm's length, at war. They begin at defeat and proceed to risk the tilt from annihilation's crown. The left one backs up against the right, stroking it, almost sexually, one on top of the other as one. Instead of looking into my face they look away, leaping into their own sense of victory, alone. Each one intimate with reckless wildness, yet acting like a two-headed madonna. Wrist of the left, broken across the table, fumes with the idea of misery and fighting between the two, a brew of flesh snarls curdle. Me Mr. Between, stripped of the broad capacity of mind to realize these are *my* hands, *my* saving idea, with the slightest jerk, could pull away. Engine piston downward pounding the right pushing the left to the rim of the table, the left hand being left at its natural end. How hold your chin up, left, in the fierce grip of right's iron five? Your standing girlish fingers curl in shyness. Run long, left wrist! There is no resisting the right one's power pressure. The ongoing struggle of two preparing for a bad way. Torture. There the left sat timidly thigh-fumbling, while the right, never grumbling, grasped hats and saluted the clouds. The left was never an arm of abuse, has never spoken words of indulgence, and yet the right has been made my favor, without my wishing the left any harm at all—why? And so I sit, escaping nothing now, chin pressed to the edge of the burnished oak table, nothing unnoticed passing before me—the brought holds of various knots, the shadow strings between palms, bunching up darkness in my eyes. My frozen gaze is never to be peeled from my hands, because they are mine! Agony must referee this match of stalled touch, one bearing more pressure on the other from left to right and back across the tabletop, fingers tangled in a locked instant. This after facing one another, palm to palm and bowing, saluting me together, now their meek referee. Referee reading a terrific book they had slammed shut, when my two hands began to fight.

MY WIGGY VIKING

is a subterranean burly node of ball lightning clustered yellow
like huddled blood. He's one pure sphere of bone—the holes
in his skull are smoothed over, are a wind-polished dome of ice.
I keep him underground until the air is ripe for garden parties.
Upon arrival he makes the guests' veins wince like a gust does,
and gives them jagged hiccups. He's by-and-large, large, by and
by. His mouth is full of tiny glaciers, he cools our drinks by
smiling into them. He keeps his ship in a small pouch around
his neck. In conversation he emphasizes a point by grabbing the
pouch and gesticulating madly with it. When he does so, salt
waves crest in our bellies and a fury of Viking blades fall from
the clouds.

THE BLUEBERRY ORACLE

Walking through the blueberry scrub, I find a bent over haggard elder mincing words in the wind-torn shrubbery, babbling forth the scraggly vernacular of the underbrush. He is screaming about blue skulls and little bent crowns off kilter. As I stand before him he turns to the sky with his fists in the air and curses the "obnoxious blue molecules." I wonder if he's not one of these smoky water droplets, evaporating like a stray idea, adrift through the dry spokes of a clock. And then I realize he's a blueberry pilgrim, hunched in praise and conversion, paying homage at The Blueberry Oracle.

A YAWN AND THE SIGN OF UNCONDITIONAL LOVE

A yawn might be used to vacuum the drapes, or stifle a windmill, or yank crinkled pale sheets off the Pacific. It is taut now, the sea like starched sheets, starched sheets taught to sing from their sheet-like lips, that drunken sailor's song, "I was six sheets to the wind, and twelve crabs to the clouds." At which point one's mouth is interrupted by a passing lightning storm, that has traipsed in off the sea. To have your mouth agape, full of electric clouds, ships passing between your interrupted teeth, this is a sign of unconditional love.

SEX TWIGS AND OTHER HUMBLE BYGONES AT THE CHURCH-PRISM OF INWARDNESS

A collage on the altar, said pastures of dreaming, late summer creosote between the feet of my nose. Sovereign breath magma punches the ice column lodged in my spine. I stand upright for a while, proud as a registered car. I have a two headed pen with thirteen personalities, one dresses up as a pencil and does prehensile duck dives into the tomato soup. The other broke down on the way to the fairgrounds, saw purpose loitering in a charcoal bathrobe by the banana hydrant. Either one will do, will sop up the forethought where memory's waist band has snapped the foreskin of intention. All forward clusters on the linoleum, line up please. Here such coral pulp traps seem to evade traction in the snow loops. Make way. Kneel in a prayerful deluge, and hum!

AMERICAN BAGGIE

A plastic grocery bag does an elegant dance against a brick wall back drop. A teenage boy gazes into its movements mesmerized by the crinkled pirouettes, its undulating sweeps, its flesh-like painterly tremblings. Up it swirls into a cadence of stars only to fall abruptly through absent breath around the boy's head. The wind cinches the bag's handles in a knot around his neck. The boy's head bloats and turns dark purple behind the ragged visage of the bag. The boy is now floating up against a brick wall backdrop in an elegant dance, in crinkled pirouettes, in undulating sweeps of flesh-like painterly tremblings.

ONE THUMB BOOK

I am building a little book for my thumb, where we will shovel lint from the street's navel and juice lullabies from the treetops. It is a book of elastic steel married to song. An opposable piano picked up in Mozambique. Each page a print, a maze of jagged feet clamoring up the stairwell of your spine. This a gnarled tornado as opposed to a combed one. This a hairy coin of sorts, the flipping of which is the fondling of crude feathers, where we memorialize the world record holder in the pole vault.

we will audit windows for the barley smear, and trickle. We'll go ahead with the frumped cottonwood, shave it for all it's empty of. Embark upon of, and its entrails on a Wednesday. Eat frigid pigeons till they get then. Then open a frog collar toward dawn. Say it's never a near miss when the whistles mend. I've fought more transient heaps than these—each one's more humble than the fog it clenches. You can't unweld the frycakes with a scratching post, so go on, onward, bother why. What's the use of. Further more use is used up. Don't count the other end in. It just keeps wilting poor Will's patience, which hasn't a ham to stand on, nor even a burped up drill bit to wield. Be oven. Be soldered. Be rendered freight cloth and unencumbered chub. Hollow out the frenzy before partitioning the urge, and tarnish. Cube the ink into seven inch circles of butane and light from within. You'll want to unglove the periodicals before cucumbering them. Keep chasing the written-on windows till they're blindsided. Heave light there. Heave wind behind you this time so it doesn't bugger the forecaster's toast. Can you blame the carbon limbs for half a green cast? It rains them once every Sunday first. What of it. Competing against the snow is a fishhook flaking off my temple. This completes the soot arrangement, and eggs me in. How can anyone train an itch, let alone peel one? Each shard is a peach hair I do the remembering with. It has a narrow hour to keep, a cage to implode thistles in, and an accomplishment claw made of divisive glass. This is the day a few ungreased hankerings leak across the housing of your lapels, where the half-life of pleasure is a growling monk.

THE CAPTAIN

He's watching pleasure, aristocratic & mysterious. He's sort of gummed-up in ambition's spool. Curiosity is all lost to the man, above all beauty, above all. Rhythm tastes alive in the man who keeps swells gracefully, so that rigging doesn't complicate the long slim lines in the ship's tops. His eye ever tiring, gladdens design, a marvelous prism forming lighthouses there. Its beams flash the sea forward, colors changing the mobile clouds, from which a sea port drops. The sky is a wide expanse of struggles, as seen by the captain.

THE TOOTH

The tooth is a hoof mistaken for a hat. The hoof in the mouth is a tongue full of wool. A woolen tongue does no good during feeding. The tooth is better for evening walks in the forbs. The hat is lost to the words in the forbs. The forbs are a long time in waiting to be eaten with the words. The man with the woolen tongue and hoof in his mouth is a long time waiting for forbs, for words. Both starve in the mean time, the meantime gives neither a thought, and the world turns once again through the trembling open mouth of the night.

BRILLIANT PEBBLES

Gordon is a physicist, he is physical, he is the epitome of National Defense. He defended the wildcats in the Lincoln Middle School football state championships in Lopsided, Illinois back in 1962. He is currently filled with brilliant pebbles— situated at the breakfast table at the Four Seasons Hotel with a couple of his colleagues. His colleagues have been to college, they are collegiate. On their days off from the lab, they make abstract collages out of magazine pictures and construction paper adhered with Elmer's glue. Gordon's brain goes tick tick with the brilliant pebbles. He wants to share his tiny stones with the boys. He opens his briefcase and a briefing falls out complete with rock dust and metallic satellite parts. His eyes are heavy with power, dark brown satchels drooping into his Eggs Benedict. "Rogue nations beware!" He shrieks at the waitress. Startled, the waitress spills hot coffee on a neighboring table scalding the Griswalds. The scalded Griswalds scowl at Gordon and the waitress while exiting stained. "Boys, my Brilliant Pebbles..." He continues, "are highly intelligent bombs that will rain down from twittering satellites and deflect enemy launches in the boost phase by thrusting missile interceptors at them. Give me the salt." He stammers, getting hard between the legs, his cheeks filling up with saliva. Colleague 1 thrusts the salt at Gordon which is intercepted by the pepper mistaken for the salt as thrust by Colleague 2. "Apricot spreadable fruit, you assholes" Gordon screams, then continues, "Imagine a dandelion head gone to seed with its white tufts launched into space against an evening sky, imagine that seed with exact eyes and a huge bullet that could deflect a stray rain drop by swatting it out of the sky, imagine glorious fireworks high within the earth's atmosphere raining multicolored sparks to the ground, in a protective rainbow halo arcing over the entire U.S. of A."

CLOCK ON THE HEAD

I wake up groggy and annoyed, hit the alarm clock with a handy bedside frying pan. The clock, upset, wrestles the handy pan from my hand, and clocks *me* on the head. I fall back, fast asleep, dead pan beside the bed.

HAIR PIECE

Memories are eating I who be rebellious hair! An elastic bellowing befalls me when beneath some heavy tresses, the long, long cocoanut oil, the thin tar and musk are smelling drunk with this hairy shoreline. It is an infinity that is blue and tropical with an uncertain sheen. Your hair is a sugary opium filled night. This, the tobacco strangled fragrance of our hair hearth breath in short.

Jars of water are cooling incensed flowers, pots between swollen imperceptibles. As the harbor is cradling fair ships in swell like watery couches lying across languid hours in a bay. Here again the knowledge of your hair caresses. Here heat is home in the sky's enormity, its outstanding intricate structure whose elegant shapes every ship and nation lug through lusty men. Oh how melancholic songs are teeming through the harbor of your hair!

Air is the perfumed skin of your head, you human leaf claiming thready fruit, you are more profound and bluer than any clime I've climbed. There are wafting monsoons for christsakes, whose seas hold sails and masts hostage, which are soon peeled from the depths of your hair. Men's souls are tangled in your hair's music. Hear all that we feel here, we feel hair singing through our finger's ears.

It's this pure air in the memory's stirring handkerchiefs scented like white rosey waves. It's me letting spring out of the water, I am a thirsty man—facing the plunge of hairy breath, and the breathy heave of memory, memory eating fragrance bare!

I HAVE A HAND

It looks like two but is one. It fits on the end of my spindle, the end of my window. It fits on the end of my shark-skin light bulb—my idea it fits on the end of my idea. My hand, it screws into the end of my bulbous idea. A bulbous fit on the end of my two front teeth, that are really just a bare tooth—a bulb, a bear tooth—grrrrrrrrrrr. One hand at the end of my tooth like a mop, oh my mop-like teeth, I will mop up my hand with my teeth, and chew forth the sky, what sky, the sky unscrewing my idea of the sky. Oh, how I have a hand.

BACKWARD FLOWERS

Strong and young roses throng the terraces, marble the sky the sea has lured in. Snowy limbs and some blue eyes are there, huge with god. Rose water surrounds rubies of delicate sprayed satin, white domelike bouquets, emerald columns supporting mahogany and agate over strewn pieces of gold. Hair, filigree, the silver eyes of a carpet, an opening, a digitalis, and the sun he is black within. This, the turning of crystal discs and fine gauzes, gray velvet, where green chords are tightening his sight.

THE TEA MAN

I happen upon the tea man who has tea leaf eye lashes and a tea leaf skirt in which he parades around the frog pond. The spring peepers are peeping at him, he peeping back. On the bank of the pond sits a Buddha statue cradled in crystals. The tea man sits there waiting for the sky to open. He peeps at the Buddha, the Buddha peeping back at him. Upset by the frigid, gray grasp of winter, he cries, and little pear blossom petals flutter from his mulchy eyes. He weeps forth spring from the fruit trees—he bats a few eyelashes, drops another petal or two, and tugs on a warm cloud. 37 drops fall into his porcelain cup. He sips, the sky parts, the frogs peep. Here & now everything crystallizes for the tea man.

THE SANCTITY OF SQUARES

"I am an ar'teest!" Insists the solitary pine man slogging around in the pine bog. He's been inserting nine pine cones in to his nine sacred holes for nine hours now. "I am a prolific pine bog performance baron!" He bellows. He has been collecting pine pollen from the dusty cones. He finds the pollen lovely and acute, troubling and sublime. He gathers it up into medium glass cages throughout the pollinating season. He snorts some, smears some on his orifice, his oracle, his organ. He gets on an airplane, gets off an airplane, pollen always in hand, intercontinental pollen. He wipes pollen in squares, on fine paper on other continents in ravishing cities. Pollen on paper in square frames from square bottles, and sprinkled in squares on concrete floors in expensive galleries, sifting it all through a muslin funnel. On the floor his pollen glows, it hovers, it vibrates, it has frayed canary-like feathery edges, a square of moonlight spilling in from the museum window. It just might peel off the floor as a solid, a pat of airborne butter, so glorious be the winged pollen.

The next day pine man is having lunch with the curator of the fine arts museum in Düsseldorf. They are lunching outside in the museum cafe, it is a lovely warm spring afternoon, the triangular pine trees in the garden are casting ominous square shadows. He bites into his croissant not noticing the bee that has crawled into its buttery folds—the man chews, the bee stings, the man spits, the man gags, his tongue flowers up like an agitated pomegranate. Breath is lost to the man. He collapses into his little boat of pollinated death, while the bee drowns in his buttery saliva, but the squares, oh, how the squares live on.

FREERANGE MEATBALLS

I went to sleep in the rain with some free range turkey meat balls at my side, in my side, inside me ranging free clucking and rolling around unconditional, circular, full of meat and freedom in my dreams. The whole night through we swam there, in the actual rain dressed in circular feathers being eventual, completely poignant, frugal, and tender—rolling free at home on the range in the rain my fleshy planets, my crumpled brown ideas, tumbling headlong out of the sun.

THE ELEVATED TOWER OF FUR

for Wll Yackulic

The elevated tower of fur is hard to resist and soft to advances. It creeps always upward as breath does sky. This, however, is not such fur worth climbing, unless your ego for hand height is way high. For every time an ascent is attempted, fistfuls of the tower come off in your palms, and forever your palms are furry, even though the elevation is sacrificed from the missing clumps. A missing fistful of this tower is the lost height of hands. Except for the belief in those hands that make repeated attempts at ascending. For some the accumulation of fur is profound. They strut around with fur towers in their palms never having to worry at the height of their hands and yet never quite reaching the handless stature of the original, elevated, tower of fur.

An iced-over man and a moss covered guy are perched on a stiff branch. One's got only half a cheek, the other, half an ear. One says to the other, "Hows bout I take yer other good ear to fill in my half cheek so I can listen to Shostakovich through my mouth. You take my good cheek to have better the chewing of fine yams."

"What, and go around with just half an ear and two cheeks piled high upon the side of my head? As it stands I can only hear three fourths, and you propose I only hear one quarter?"

"No no," quips iced-over man, "I give you twice the cheek for the immaculate staving off of slaps to the face we get from being mossed and iced and a feature short to the face."

"Hmm," peeps moss covered guy hunching a bit on the branch, "You know how I'm not a fan of yams and how swapping features makes me queasy at this height, and furthermore it fuels the ears for their flight toward the sun."

"Precisely," insists iced-over man, "What better way to be so strewn in this frigid kingdom of exchange?"

ONE OUT THE WINDOW

Night through skittering air, tumbles and rolls, chased I as trees slipping for it, it's reach reached I, as a lighted room does climb me through it. To want it, to see that I am wind in the paper, a piece of night, slipping through floating windows, where the lighted ones go.

WHEN THE SAYING WAS UNVEILED

When the saying was unveiled what was said remained unavailable. Fred However said, get the snowy egret can opener at once and open wide of its hexagonal feathers. Lana's saying was hitched to crushed brushes, bent bristles protruding from her tongue. She was a painter before the colors stalled mid-flight. Gary hated being vague, said, film was whale skin mistaken for a veil, and that it blocked out Being altogether. But someone needed someone's blubber for their lamp & guiding. Their lamp & guiding in turn said many chubby things of shadow on the stark walls of the fish shack. The fish shack was inhabited with blubber-hungry gnomes chatting about where to shit when the snows came seaside. The gnomes coming seaside said, excrement, sandal, frost depth, and willow-trowel. Things alighted then in their saying and the world arose. The willow trowel alighted toward the frost and was useful, was deep. The veil was faded with the further saying and the egrets feathers further quieted the world.

THE HOG TOOTHED MOUNTAIN TOP

Dishes of silver on an inflated balloon, where a helium drunk maitre d' serves an immense blown up buffet. Snowy mountains from waters mix with powders and grains to form food climbing mountains. I whip out my map to double check my location, the universe, through itself, is staring headlong into me. Oh mighty interest of mine, the universe, great witness of awareness I am through it frankly nothing, frankly everything, frankly frankly, hello frankly— what others could have been chosen over me, none others, I trust it's their failures, that reflect my own, my own, own. The precautions toward climbing take duty to task in falling carefully, as we do, being true to that I am. How mountainous a top it is frankly, life, my wasting away on-going in the midst of deciding so quickly about my dying, my living, my frog tough wing-nut effluvium and the crawling across mountainous planks in which discovery is emblazoned upon the floorboards. These words imprinted in my kneecaps. "Oh great hog-toothed mountain top, I come to you through silver dishes, blind to height and humble to altitude."

ANASAZI 49TH STREET

for Bill Berkson

When I walk down 49th Street in New York City, I imagine a canyon. I look into a west-side window and see sandstone towers reflected in the distance. I turn around and see a chain-link fence and an empty lot, (a woven basket against the sky) and a beige brick high-rise. I stare into the beige brick and see a sandstone cliff-dwelling on the opposite side of the street. The opposite side of the street is strewn with pottery shards and glass. The pottery shards are cockroach backs, and in among the shards of glass, I see my skin. I see a shark in the shards of my skin, and let out a scream. Then I see the scream in a three piece suit floating before my eyes like a contorted puff of blue smoke. I swat it with my briefcase, and it disappears into a shroud of sound (cockroaches skittering across the cement), a Volkswagon Beetle is tearing down the street—one of the old ones—echoing through the canyon.

HER TONGUE TRAIPSES ZERO

Her tongue traipses zero over the edge of a dune. The desert seamstress's eye is woven to heat. She had been waiting for a suit black with needles and pins, some feelings toward the depth of him. Him being a blue empty region of sand, a sculptured stranger impersonating kitchen noises. Him startles the girl, spectral in her blackened voyage. Him just a dissonant epic of grains. She being seen from the grain with a sandy expanse to sew across, and some wayward ladles to keep her company.

God on everyone, bless god!! Writes, will I say man? Belch! I belch on my writing! Says god, I belch on the man. You will sun his saying over father over dinner says father—dinner over all wrote over the man—QUEL SOUFFLÉ Dinner over all, wrote the man again—dinner comes to the people! These are all the leavings I can stand, said mother, alone. Bearing exhaustion is one, said mother said father, said god. Father on father writes he, as I sayeth the man. There are many too many gods at work writing mother and father senseless for their sun, their son. Which instance is first in the too-many world? The too-many world, with too many sons writing, it's having, like, redundancy for dinner, no?? Stop stop stop, said father with his written on foot stuck in his written on mouth stuck in his written on god. Each hand his forehead his forehead, each hand his forehead, writing forth his hand hand forehead, oh god, say man no more, but that parts make me whole.

MRS. WESTWARD FACING MUSTACHE

Mrs. Westward Facing Mustache twitched her upper lip and bowed into a nearby cloud, cloud going haywire on the pyrotechnic horizon. A raging orange and blue sunset arose from the sea and then drowned in lost air. Bleak blue light flowered over the land, spoke to bent creek and crick-in-the-rock. Both said no wind, squirmed between breaths but let the black sky spread and little flint babies parade. Silver flint babies born out of saying were airborne in strange patterns, forming bear, coyote, and raven-over-head. The three of them gave birth to themselves and descended the night sky staircase to greet Mrs. Westward Facing Mustache. They gathered in the tall grass quivering of her busy upper lip and got cozy before the fire. They called it fire-out-of-chalk-teeth, they called it smoke-from-snake-tongue—Mrs. Westward Facing Mustache told us stories round the fire.

FRANKIE IN THE TOMBS

Frankie used to dangle a gold chain between his broken gold teeth. You could hear the three-inch crucifix at the end of it clanking between his bent gold molars. He threatened to swallow it if we didn't let him drive the warden's car to score some chutney in Jackson Heights. Good Friday in '92 he went ahead and swallowed it—he passed it through on Easter Sunday.

THEY TIMES THEY EQUALS THEM

for Lisa Jarnot

They had earthquakes in their cake pans and a stand of Quaking Aspens fixed in the belly of their cakes. They had closets in the folds of the golden Aspen leaves, timid closets, closets the size of a quick yawn— this is where they kept their shimmerings. Their shimmerings were hooded and spoke in a rural and maniacally fragrant, chartreuse drawl. They had baby spinach church lights caught in their teeth. They had wounded minutes in copper strands gasping at the backs of their necks. They gave grave speeches about jellyfish wranglers in the North Sea. They gave dark gray speeches about graves. They worked the bleach white graveyard shift as outreach coordinators showing examples of their humble hands. They multiplied in splendid little roadside mirrors, from hand to mouth to palm and back. And that's where they fell, they, finally upon them.

CANTALOUPE ARMS

Last night I saw a pair of vultures—one feeding on the remains of my neighbor—the other crouched and waiting in the notch of an ancient white oak. I strolled by curiously eyeing the feeding, keeping my carnage to myself, when one vulture tore himself loose from the carcass and followed *me* down the road. He swooped nearer with an air of aggression, and rose to a size of a classic black zeppelin. I turned abruptly, swatting and stomping, thinking I might frighten him away. He merely laughed, loomed higher, and lunged toward me, his wings now soaking up most of the night.

Now, I had been walking back from the farm and was armed with two quite ripe cantaloupe. My last thought was to beam him with the melons. The first one I hurled went straight at his face, splitting in half against his beak, pale seeds and mucusy orange strands dripping off his shrivelled head. The second melon missed him entirely, breaking apart on the ground, rolling into small pieces. Empty of arms, I scrambled to a nearby oak and shimmied up the branchless trunk, until I got to a notch where I just crouched and waited.

PELICANESQUE

An ornery billed pelican crosshatches the edible dawn. Some clansmen arrive to swat tufa spires with their porcelain chins. Digestible mouths spool forth cooler air, as their breath is said brittle upon the sea. It's breakfast before the book, and a hen is already dwarfed in the thistle stands. I'm writing from a landscape equipped with Harlequin earholes. I'm embarking upon autumn with a numb glove. Today I saw one biplane with my bifocals hoping for four. What's become of the scene before me—subject to the deliberate high-caliber Framboise? One lofty doughnut after the next is corralled into ether. No access for even a hole. Such cyclical text will exit into the splendid gilded coronary noon. One step forward during that hour and you're doomed. Doomed to a week full of peacock tea-cakes and outbreaks of the rickets. Brainstorms stay inside and thumb their noses at the fop. They further plunder tofu congregations while redefining the cabbage, so it's no longer just ashen strands, but strands the length of my favorite ancestor. My favorite ancestor an ornery bird, and this his ancestral command.

HEART'S DREAM

Thinkin' then how the thick thought hobbled upstream through sage knots and granite webs looking for its heart's dream. None too soon had the thought happened upon Mrs. Not-Cottonwood and asked, "Can you tell me the where of my heart's dream, what color might it be—perhaps a bulbous crimson, like the stain-dense liver of wolves?" "Bah—lost thought," said Mrs. Not-Cottonwood, "go drown in the white shampoo of the milky way." there you might find your heart's dream, sentenced to a life in ink." "Hmmm," thought the thought, bending its vaporous neck over the reflecting waters of the stream, the night sky. "Speak, oh slinky urine of the stars—where might my thin heart's dream grow obese?" the thought asked the stream. "Bah—go bang your thoughtful head upon the hectic brow of a veiny boulder,"spake the stream. "Hmmm" thought the thought, its synapse tangling, ready to head-butt a nearby stone. "Oh gracious stone, speak to me of my heart's dream," said the thought, rubbing a sizeable head-wound, smearing wolve's-liver paste all over it's face. "Double bah," said the boulder, "look no further than the sage sting between your thoughtful nostrils." "Ahh," said the thought, taking a deep breath, its nostrils now glowing pale green and fragrant, standing up spiny in the lavender moonlight. . ..

COPS ON THE FARM

Stars and hay, the smell of moonlight in the policeman's rusting pistols, tarnished badges, spent earth. They term it themselves, call it "The Chicken Perch Monotony." Taking the hen out of the house is just asking for the police, cries the farmer. "Chickens, are you chickens, are you police?" Cow and farmer have been called to chaperone the police toward the farmer's kisses. Being shy though they are, through bellowing mouths and tongues of the rolling cow, cow being cow with slick cud kissing, was the farmer's idea of freedom. The cops thought not, but soon were engendered as love seeps in lieu of their dissolving modesty. Such was the assault upon pleasant bellowing and bad extremes of the cow's voice against the window sill. They are species between commerce, them cop & cow-dung-dude-farmers. Their milk comes by way of married men—cow raptured to man to cow to man, in little milky satellites around the moon. "The moon is the mustard sister" says the policeman, waxing poetic in the condiments. "My thoughts, oh my thoughts of bone from the hat—remove the farmer from his love song, his cow singing toward him with moonlit udders—and you have removed the smell of the policeman's rusting stars, his sturdy chicken perch—and what's left is a lonely farmer and heaps of tarnished badges in the spent hay."

AGELESS IN SLEEP

River, on a tree, in a tangled corpse, branches, dark and high, through floating stars, where an old porous man like shaped clouds, fields some white in the moon's many liftings. Absurd and boneless nature, his first moon, is frosty sperm in a meadow like a silver pool. The door, back under his cheek, from which a downward tear is moving, is like a floor yet drips wax beads where gravity is flattened by lies and boundaries. Aware no longer, no body, man is ancient when asleep.

WALKING THE DOG

I'm off to walk the dog this morning, when I notice my hat's on fire. I run upwards, trying to flag down a saturated cloud. No luck. The fire spreads into my scalp and head, starting a smoldering root fire in my cranium. I think "Wow, like accelerated honey shed from the core of the sun." No matter, the dog must be walked. "No fire as mad as the unwalked dog!" I insist into the clever flames, flesh bubbling up, popping off bone. Late for work, I continue on, soon finding me walking an ashen self on an ashen leash, the neighbors asking ashen questions, the dog barking forth some ashen answers.

THE ORIGINS OF FORM

A man stumbles out of a meteor shower lit up with love and answers, his hair tossed back with fire. His tie is singed, and flaking ash all over the sidewalk as he returns to the streets of Manhattan a changed man. He steps into a luncheonette hungry from his travels, and immediately the entire staff and customers gather around and begin pelting him with questions worse than any asteroid. They are demanding answers as to the origins of form. His first answer is to the waitress to whom he says, "I'd love a B.L.T. and a large iced tea."

THE OPPOSITE DIRECTION

Not quite awake I reach in to my closet mirror mistaking it for the rack of clothes, and bang my hand against the muted reflection. The mirror comes off in my hand like mercurial thought, in the form of a silver muslin jump-suit. So I jump right in, wear it to work. It's a perfect fitting skin yet no one recognizes me, they just see themselves replicated in exact animation and run screaming in the opposite direction. Even the opposite direction freaks out screaming, though stays where it is. There is no one left in this direction, I am alone as a mirror to the world.

THE CREEK

Every day I go to the creek. I marvel at its beauty, its silvery ripples that never tangle, its black velvet chasms that rarely swallow anything but light. I stare into it as if to see myself liquefied and transparent melting into the soil. I am so fond of the creek, that I wish to take it with me when I leave. So I do, I pick it up gently from the center, careful not to spill, and toss it around my neck like a thorough Anaconda. It fits comfortably and stays put. Back at the house I look into the mirror and find my new adornment to be quite stylish. I tie the creek around my neck, as I would a necktie and go about my day. In town my new fashion statement turns thirsty heads and garners a spongy crowd, all who want to draw from my neck a cool drink. So I loosen my tie, right there in the street, and lean into their curious tongues.

THE WAKING

A man places a glass of water on his bedside table. He crawls into bed falling rapidly asleep. He dreams he's in the desert and dying of thirst. Alarmed, he wakes sweating and covered in sand like a freshly breaded breast of chicken. He gazes around the room, seeing sand dunes strewn across the carpet, a kit fox barking orders from behind a volcanic stone, a withered thorn tree where the kitchen once was. The sun pours through the dilapidated roof beams scorching his now bald head. Bewildered, he pinches his sandy skin. A small trickle of blood wriggles between sand grains from the small patch of torn skin. He screams, and several desert sparrows dart forth from his breath. He screams again, more sparrows. He keeps screaming till an umbrella of sparrows forms above his head, blocking out the sun. He follows the flock of screams around his desert bedroom, and out across the dunes. Tortured by thirst, he goes madly in search of his glass of water. He runs off chirping after the horizon, begging for his bedside table, for his glass of water. Exhausted, he pauses and looks behind him to notice that the horizon is now chasing him. He stops, anticipating its approach. The horizon behind him arrives before him, with that tall glass of water in its horizontal hand. "WAKE UP ASSHOLE!!" shouts the horizon, pouring the glass of water over the parched man's head, smashing the glass in the sand at his feet, and then stammers off into the distance of its own making.

HEAVEN HAS LAYERS

Some mysterious surgeons with silent hands showed up at the factory one day. I blacked out with fear being held in some chasm of water turned to fire. There were murmurings of invisible animals I questioned, and then laughter rang out from the lava swamp. What can I say of the factory basement, the less-than-beautiful sight of me coming to, in flames. Rising up through the office, past shipping & handling, the public area, reception, all less pretty than the previous layers. I rise, the surgeons follow, chasing me with clacking scalpels and hoods of dark gauze—through all the layers I hated to work. And so I had stolen an umbrella, to catch a warm updraft, rising toward the ceiling like an unpeeled scar, into the umbrella-shaped skylight, and out of the grasp of the crimson surgeon's hands.

THE CHUCKLING SKY

Here comes fear lurching down the trail, cocksure, with a fierce strut, snapping passing branches. He's got metal spikes in his thorny beard and pitchfork-claws tangling up the innocent air. He's shouting biblical epithets at the agnostic clouds, stirring forth an anticipatory story of blooming gloom. His wrath is that of gangly anger, angling toward more future fire. Fear's face bleats blood-red drops, acts like impatient flame, glaring briefly—briefly trailing off into the chuckling sky.

FROM SEA COME WOMAN, COME MAN

Beneath a ten-point sprocketed sun, a pair of salt-creased hands crack down the middle, a palm-sized stone. The broken edges left between their splitting is the profile of a woman's back-lit night-black body. Her body narrows downward to a point at the bottom of the stone. The stone floats on the horizon, is cradled by bright hands, blurs misty in an inkish sea. The trailing reflection of the sun upon this sea blends into a frothy white human shadow streaming toward land, this time man, foaming forward in kissing shapes, arising as one in waves upon the shore.

MY PLANE

My plane is huge, it is transcontinental, it hugs the sphere way up high. When in flight my plane averages 541 mph at an altitude of 37,000 feet. This makes me nervous, makes me need a Valium the size of a hubcap, to calm me down upon my plane. The pilot of my plane wears a leopard skin headdress and cranks Frank Sinatra on the Victrola over the intercom. The distortion is excruciating. The fuselage of my plane is made of deer meat hanging in the sun's arms. We are fed venison with our mixed nuts. My plane is very gamey. The stewardi on my plane are French homoerotic economists. They turn me on, then kindly turn me off, for a small fee. My plane has one overhead compartment. It is named sky. All of my luggage fits in there. My plane has several emergency exits for my safety—both fore and aft, and just in case, I sit both fore and aft, looking forward to the emergency, wondering what I'll do afterward. In the event of a water landing I feel confident that I can be directed by a crew member to do the backstroke, butterfly, or doggie paddle. The miniature bottles of spring water are to be used as a floatation device. Upon lift-off on my plane all of my nerves smolder before my very eyes in the seat pocket in front of me, fizzling out into the recirculated air. While in the lavatory I experience turbulence and bang my head against the smoke detector. The stewardi on my plane accuse me of tampering. They smell the funny smoke of smoldering nerves upon my clothes, and instead of arresting me, force me out into the harsh crust of our cruising altitude. They lead me out blindfolded midflight, to the end of our de-iced wing. There they let me off somewhere above Assisi, freeing me from my plane and the ideas I have created about it.

About the Author

Albert Flynn DeSilver was born in Connecticut in 1968. He received a BFA in Photography from the University of Colorado and an MFA in New Genres from the San Francisco Art Institute. He is the author of *Letters to Early Street* (La Alameda Press, 2007), *Ageless in Sleep* (Angry Dog Midget Editions, 2002), Some Nature (D-Press/The Nonexistent Press, 2001/2004) and many other books and chapbooks. He has published more than one hundred poems in literary journals throughout the U.S. and abroad including *New American Writing, Zyzzyva, Hanging Loose, Volt, Lungfull!, Jacket, Chain, Van Gogh's Ear* (Paris), and *Poetry Kanto* (Japan). He teaches with California Poets in the Schools and The Stepping Stones Project in Northern California.

Other books and chapbooks by Albert Flynn DeSilver

Letters to Early Street (La Alameda Press, 2007)

dismissiles/rains (The Nonexistent Press, 2006)

Working Title (The Nonexistent Press, 2005)

Some Nature (D-Press/The Non Existent Press, 2001/2004)

Ageless in Sleep (Angry Dog Midget Editions, 2002)

Time Pieces (The Owl Press, 2001)

A Pond (TOP, 2001)

Al & Marian's Coast to Coast Roundup (TOP, 2000)

Foam Poems (TOP, 1998)

Ten Sea Birds (TOP, 1998)

albeit (TOP, 1998)

The Book of Not (TOP, 1997)